The Passive Income Playbook: How Alternative Investments Can Help You Get Rich and Retire Early

Copyright ©2017 Lancaster Chatham Publishing

What if you could get higher returns for lower risk? Would you take it? The stock market is great for growing your capital over the long term, but it isn't the only game in town. Many, many millionaires have been made with smart investments in real estate, private businesses, and other alterative investments. This book is about showing you how to take advantage of each of these opportunities, which can supplement or replace stock market investing and make you rich. Passive income has life changing benefits for those who earn it, and you can do much better than dividend paying stocks when it comes to passive income. So if passive income is your goal, you need to look at alternatives to a traditional stock and bond portfolio.

Inside:

- How you can get started investing in real estate, the world's first great creator of wealth, even if you don't have a big down payment.
- How peer-to-peer investment platforms change the investing game, giving you access to consumer loans, real estate partnerships, and hard money loans.
- How real estate can reduce your taxes.
- How you can refinance your properties to buy even more property, effectively cloning your investments.

- How to select businesses that you can buy and run semi-absentee, giving you round the clock income, and more.

You can get rich, retire early, dump the 9-5, and live the life you want. What you need is some real world education on how alternative investing works, and how to get rich.

Is the Stock Market the Best Place to Invest?

The media tells you that if you have some extra money to invest, the best place to put that money is in the stock market. After all, that's how Warren Buffett got rich, right? As anyone who had money in the market during the 2008 financial crisis can attest, the stock market is not a smooth ride all the time. Stocks fell over 50 percent peak to trough, and a lot of investors panicked and sold.

A lot more people than you think panicked and sold during the fall of 2008 leading into the bottom of that market in March 2009. I feel for them. Nobody should have to work their whole life, saving up money and doing everything right, only to lose it all with one bad decision to sell at the bottom of a catastrophic bear market. I think everyone knows someone who has lost some money in the stock market. The stories go like this, "My friend lost 100k investing in their friend's biotech company, or so and so bought into a hot technology stock that ended up being on the wrong side of the market." Usually in these stories there is some element of doubling down involved, often after an investment has gone sour, people double down, investing money they really can't afford to lose in a bad stock. I'm here to tell you that if you know someone who has lost money in the market, or are close with someone who has, forgive them, or forgive yourself if you were the one who lost. The market is a psychological roller coaster, and the truth is that many people have a difficult time making money in the stock market. **In fact, the stock market can be psychological hell.** Personally, I am a person who is very logical, and I'm in a good place financially, so I like the stock market, and fully understand that it goes down sometimes but the risk justifies the reward. I also like alternatives to the stock market, because I like to have multiple income streams and I like to hedge my bets. When you invest in different assets that aren't correlated with each other, you greatly increase the chance of making money in any given year, month, week or day.

The stock market might not be for you if:

- **You have a tendency to panic when the market falls sharply**, which it does do on average every 5-7 years. The stock market is a profitable investment for most people. If you have lost money in stocks over more than a 3-4 year period, the stock market probably isn't for you.
- **You like to take a more hands-on role in your investments.** The fact is that the management and employees of large

corporations soak up a large portion of the profits for themselves. If you don't mind doing some of the legwork yourself, enjoy working with others, and want control over your money, than you probably would be better off looking at alternatives to stocks.

- **You want more leverage than stocks allow.** The stock market and borrowed money are not a good combination for everyone. However, most people are familiar with how mortgages work, and how business loans work. The fact is that you can get a lot more long term leverage investing in private businesses or real estate than you can in stocks.

Even if you have the kind of personality well suited to the stock market, you can improve your returns and lower your risk by diversifying into other investments, as you will see.

The Wide World of

Investments

Where else can you put your money besides the stock market? Under your mattress is the first thought for many people when they have extra money, but putting money under the mattress doesn't earn any return. The best places besides stocks to put your money, in my opinion, are:

- **Real estate.** Where do you think the government wants you to invest? If you look at their policies, I would say that the government wants you to invest in real estate. If you can afford it, you want to own your own home. The reason why is that when you rent, the money that you pay goes towards paying off someone else's mortgage. Your landlord can and will raise the rent on you whenever they are between contracts, because they own the place and you don't. Just like sometimes the smartest investment move you can make is to pay off high interest debt, they first step to getting in on the real estate game is to own your own housing. It's much better, financially speaking, to "rent" from a bank via a mortgage than rent from a landlord via rent. However, if you want to make passive income investing in real estate, you need cash flow. Renting your property out is how you get passive income machine to start working in your favor. Real estate is THE place to look if you want to get consistent double-digit returns.

- **Peer to Peer Investments-** Websites like Prosper, Lending Club, Realty Shares, and PeerStreet allow you invest in loans and real estate projects with much less money than you would need otherwise. Instead of needing tens or hundreds of thousands of dollars to get started, you can get started with as little as a few hundred to a few thousand. Lending Club and Prosper allow small investors to make loans to other consumers via crowdfunding. Realty Shares, and PeerStreet allow small investors to get in on a pipeline of real estate deals that traditionally have had six figure minimum investments. This new crowd funded model makes it possible for small investors to get access to high return real estate deals or loans, and also allows developers in need of capital to quickly get funding. This is a win-win for both sides, and is truly a disruptive business model to the status quo. The best part about this for you is that the returns are high, safe, and predictable. We will cover each one of these platforms later in detail.

- **Semi-absentee businesses.** Those of you who run a more time intensive business may groan when you read this, but semi-absentee businesses have made more millionaires by the truckload. There are really two kinds of businesses in this world. The first kind is the kind that needs a sharp owner to be CEO, coach, and quarterback. The other kind is the kind that can be run by an 18-year old kid, because, well, that's your demographic for minimum wage retail jobs. Examples of businesses that need a great quarterback are bars, restaurants, car dealerships, and anything with a lot of inventory. These are also the businesses that everyone cautions you against starting because they tend to take over your life. If you want a business that you can pay someone to run while you enjoy the profits, you need to follow a few criteria. Businesses that have a license they can lose easily (liquor stores), are inventory intensive (restaurants and car dealers come to mind), or have lots of receivables (anything manufacturing) are not passive or semi-passive businesses. You want businesses that make money while you sleep, or you can pay someone else to run without too much risk of them destroying it. Good examples of semi-absentee businesses are car washes, laundromats, real estate with a property manager, authority websites, book publishing ;), and similar businesses.

These are all good examples of places you can invest your money without the constant drama of having your assets marked to market on your brokerage screen. If passive income is your goal, these investments are your solution.

Real Estate

Real estate is the oldest means of getting rich in the world. Back in roman times, landlords owned big blocks of tenements (apartments), rented them out, used the money to build more, and became some of the richest people in the empire. The reason? Everyone needs a place to live. They didn't have Fannie Mae or Bank of America back then, but people invested in real estate and got rich. What has changed in the last 2,000 years in real estate? Not much, except maybe the apartments look different. Real estate is a great investment, but instead of telling you, I'll show you. Residential real estate pretty much went straight up in value from 1970 to 2007, when the housing bubble popped. Real estate is nowhere near being in a bubble in 2017, except maybe in San Francisco and the Bay Area. The graph on top is home prices since 1970; the graph on bottom is the stock market since 1990. The comparison isn't meant to be exactly equivalent, but what you should take away from it is that stocks are much more volatile than real estate.

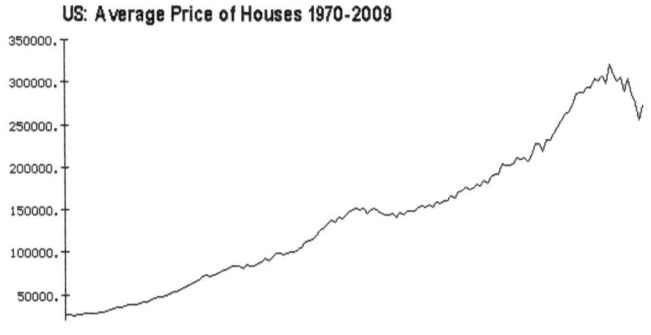

US: Average Price of Houses 1970-2009

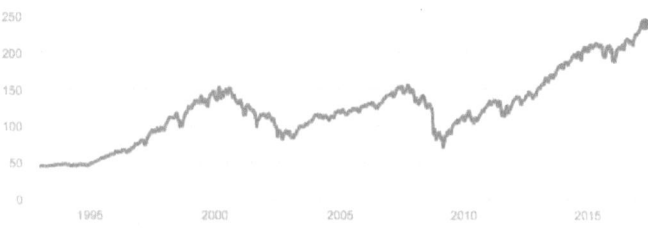

Investing in real estate has steadier returns than stocks, which means two things to you. First off, you are allowed to use a higher amount of leverage when you buy real estate. Instead of putting 50 percent down on stocks like you would if you bought on margin, or 100 percent if you pay cash, you can put 10-25 percent down on real estate purchases, depending on what you bank requires. If you qualify for an FHA loan, you can put as little as 3.5 down, giving you an amazing 28 times leverage on your investment. If you qualify for a VA loan, you can put 0 percent down, and only have to pay a loan fee of a couple percent or so.

You don't have to have perfect credit score to get an FHA loan either. Even if your score is around 600 you can get a loan from the FHA. You have to meet certain requirements, such as having the payment be less than 30-35 percent of your income, and actually occupying the house, but if your finances are in order, you basically just have to sign on the dotted line and be able to make the payments. For example, if you are able to make 70,000 dollars per year and have a 11,000 dollar down payment, you can buy a 300,000 dollar house with an FHA loan. That right there is the American dream. Owning your own home has a benefit to you also in that it functions as somewhat of a forced savings plan, as each month, a fraction of your payment goes towards shrinking your mortgage. If you ever want to move, you will have your down payment and more waiting for you in home equity.

Your mortgage will only shrink if you make your payments, it will never get bigger. **Your property, on the other hand will appreciate in value by 2-4 percent per year on average, increasing your equity when you sell.** Real estate ownership is the key to going from middle class to being considered wealthy.

Where things start to get interesting is when you use an FHA loan to acquire a multi unit property. FHA loans are allowed for not only single-family homes, but also for duplexes, triplexes, and fourplexes. A potentially very savvy move if you are young and have a decent income is to buy a property with 3-4 units, live in one and rent out the other units. If you do it right, i.e. by buying a property below market and improving the value so that you can rent it for more, the other 2-3 people will pay your mortgage and put a little money in your pocket, and you get to live for free. The FHA lets you count some of your income from renting the property to help you qualify for these types of loans. The game plan is to buy a property, fix it up, rent it out, and cash in big on the appreciation, rent, and mortgage amortization. Then, when you want to move, you refinance the property using the income from the property, and you own an investment property and you can buy another home for yourself. As you continue to save money, you will be able to buy more property using the income that you already have from your main sources of income, such as your job, and your investment income, which comes from your properties.

You can actually clone your properties by refinancing them, cashing out, and using the money for down payments on other properties. Since you are allowed to put less than 10-20 percent down, and since real estate is cash flow positive, if you do it right, you can make a lot of money in a hurry.

Investing in real estate is an excellent way to build wealth, because your return comes from four different components. The four components of your return are:

1. Rent. When you own real estate that you don't need to occupy, you can rent it out. As long as the rent you receive is greater than

your mortgage and expenses, you have a cash flow positive property. Your mortgage will never grow if you make the payments, and your expenses should be easy to budget for as long as you don't ignore them, so you should be able to easily turn a profit on property that you own. The numbers back this up, and as of 2017, it is cheaper to own a property than to rent in 42 states out of 50. Even if you think your market is cheaper to rent than own you can still find property below market that you can improve the value of by making renovations, so you should be able to turn a profit regardless. Also, you need to consider the fact that rents rise over time, whereas mortgages stay fixed. So, over time, it will be cheaper to own in all 50 states based on normal rent growth patterns. The profit that you will earn from renting real estate is expressed as your capitalization rate. Capitalization rates, or cap rates for short, are simply the rent divided by how much the property is worth. For example, if a property is worth a million dollars and rents for 75,000 dollars gross and clears 50,000 after repairs, property taxes and insurance, your cap rate is 5 percent. If your mortgage rate is 3.75 percent, then you are paying your mortgage and putting money in your pocket every month. That is a good deal for you! Cap rates tend to be higher for riskier properties, so be careful, but generally you want to see cap rates that cover your mortgage, plus a 20-25 percent margin of safety. You never want to own a property that takes more money to carry than you earn, that is how you end up broke. Real estate is harder to screw up than stocks, but you need to run the numbers and make sure that your investment is safe and has enough margin to pay your mortgage.

2. Property Appreciation. This is how you make the big money in real estate, but you don't necessarily want to rely on appreciation to make a profit on any given deal. Cash flow is the cake, but appreciation is the icing. If you own this same million-dollar property for 5 years and it appreciates at 3 percent compounded

annually, you should be able to sell for 1,159,000 dollars, netting you a capital gain of 159k over that 5-year period. If you look back to the earlier graph, you will see that this is a likely outcome if you own good real estate. You never want to rely on it, but there is a 95+ percent chance that you will be able to sell for more than you bought for if you wait long enough. Property appreciation can also depend on where you are. If your market is hot, like parts of Texas and Colorado are in 2017, then you are likely to experience property appreciation. If you are buying real estate somewhere with a perpetually weak economy, like Ohio or Michigan, then you need to make sure that your cash flow provides you enough return, because real estate tends to appreciate much more in hot economies.

3. Mortgage amortization. Every time you pay your mortgage, a little money is subtracted from your balance that you owe. Over time, as your mortgage shrinks, you own more and more equity in your property. This obviously means that you will net more on the sale after you pay off the loan. Property appreciation pulls your equity up, and paying down the mortgage pulls the amount that you owe down. Your net worth increases like clockwork, and you end up a winner. Also, if interest rates fall, you can refinance your mortgage and pay a lower interest rate, further improving your cash

flow. There are so many ways to win in real estate that it isn't even funny. In the stock market, there are so many negative possibilities coming at you from all over the world, in real estate you have a much higher degree of control. It really doesn't take a ton of skill to buy property and hold it as long as your rent exceeds your mortgage you end up a winner. If you have skill in renovation, you can increase the value of your property much more, but you too will benefit from the gentle push that mortgage amortization gives you.

4. Paper Write Offs. In the real world, you can't just claim nonexistent expenses and take a write off for them. Fortunately, real estate is not the real world as far as the US

government is concerned. If you own residential property, which is what we are discussing, you can take a write off for the total value of your buildings (not the land though) over 27.5 years. Assuming the value of the land is about 20 percent of the total value, which is typical of most markets, you can take a paper loss on your taxes for about 30,000 dollars per year, for 27.5 years. Does this mean that you can't deduct the cost of repairs? Hell no, this just is Uncle Sam thanking you for investing in real estate by not making you pay taxes. If your cap rate is 6 percent and your mortgage interest is 4 percent, and you have 20 percent equity in your property, then the way the math works out is that you end up with a profit of about 30,000 dollars in terms of cash flow, and you end up with a loss of about 2,000 dollars for tax purposes. The government does recapture the depreciation when you sell, but they give you a great loophole so that you can avoid paying taxes altogether.

Real estate is truly a gold mine when it comes to reducing your taxes. If you cash out a property and want to buy another one, you can use a 1031 exchange (google it) to buy another property of equal or greater value, and avoid paying taxes on the sale. This won't work for every situation, but it will work for most, and the 1031 exchange is a valuable thing to have in your toolbox as a real estate investor. Why? Because Uncle Sam likes you, that's why!

If you want to get started investing in real estate, you need to find properties to buy. You can find properties either on the MLS, which a real estate agent can help you do, you can buy properties at auction, or you can buy directly from interested owners. I would recommend that you buy properties that have either just come on the MLS very recently, or buy at auction. The reason why is that if a property has a good return, usually someone will try to buy it. If no one has tried to buy it, then it probably isn't a good deal. Alternatively, you can offer low prices at either an auction or to properties on the MLS, but you need to be prepared for the vast majority of your offers to be rejected. If they aren't, however, you know you are getting a good deal! Negotiation is paramount to your real estate investment success, as is keeping fees low. You want to brush up on the art of negotiation when you start your real estate journey.

Investing in real estate is a fantastic way to build wealth, but if you don't have enough money to get in yet, there is still hope. You can invest in real estate with much less money than you otherwise could by using peer-to-peer platforms, and you also can get access to lucrative markets such as credit card and debt consolidation loans too!

Peer to Peer Investment

Let's say you want to benefit from investing in real estate but you don't yet have the money you need to buy a place as an investment property yet. If it were 10 years ago, you would just have to wait until you had saved up enough money and had a long enough credit history to buy an investment property. Now, things are different. Peer to peer investing platforms make it much easier to invest in real estate, consumer loans, and really anything that has a high minimum investment. You might not have 50k for a down payment on a place, but if you had 10 friends each with 5,000 you could buy the place together, at least in theory. In practice, P2P platforms like Realty Shares and Peer Street work like having a bunch of friends who also invest in real estate. You don't know them, you don't work with them, but your capital is pooled with theirs when you invest in a project you like. What P2P investing can really do for you is to open up a whole world of alternative investments that you couldn't access otherwise with double-digit returns.

P2P investing is unique because it gives you more control over the investments that you choose than the stock market. For example, when you sign up for *Realty Shares*, a leading P2P investment platform, you are presented with a pipeline of real estate deals that you can invest in. You can choose to invest in hard money loans, which are loans secured by the real estate, or you can participate in the projects themselves. Everything is presented to you in the due diligence process, and you can see a great deal about the property, which you can use to determine whether you want to invest. Before the investments even get to you, they have to pass through Realty Shares' own due diligence process, which disqualifies a lot of obviously bad investments. The minimum investment currently is 5,000 dollars, which compared to other real estate projects is a low entry point. These kinds of investments have always existed, but until now, they had six figure minimum investments and were run by private equity people. The returns are really good. The hard money loans are returning from 8 to 12 percent, and the equity projects are returning 11-18 percent. If these numbers sound high, it's because you aren't used to doing private investments. Skilled managers are capable of hitting 18 percent more often than not with a little leverage involved. Of course, all the leverage is nonrecourse, so you can't lose more than you put in initially, and depending on the project, you should see some cash back starting about 6-12 months after you invest in a joint venture deal and from 1-6 months after you loan money in a hard money deal. 99+ of investments in these platforms are making money; the only downside is you're your money is tied up in the meantime. The point is that the biggest weakness of the stock market is also its biggest strength. **When you invest in real estate, one of the downsides is that you can't liquidate quickly. However, not being able to liquidate quickly is also the biggest strengths of real estate investing. It makes it significantly harder to make bad decisions.** Instead of the volatile graph of the stock market, Realty Shares investments tend to look more like a straight line. If you invest in hard money loans, the developers make a substantial down payment, and have to pay the interest on time according to the schedule, often on a monthly basis. If they don't pay, you and the other lenders simply take the keys, change the locks and sell the property to someone else for a discount. Realty Shares handles that part for you, and your realistic worst-case scenario is simply that it takes longer to get your money back than you expected.

Peer Street is a lot like Realty Shares, except that the only investments on the platform currently are loans. They have a solid pipeline of projects coming in, and when combined with Realty Shares, should provide enough of pipeline for new investment cash at any given time. Peer Street has a very strong track record of investment success. There are other real estate peer to peer investment platforms but I recommend these two for a few reasons. They are:

- Bankruptcy remote structure. In the freak event that the platforms you invest in go bankrupt, your investments are held separately in a different company that has the sole purpose of holding loans. Some commentators have raised concerns that if peer-to-peer platforms are run poorly and go bankrupt, you investments will be unaffected. I don't worry a ton about this, but it defeats the purpose of peace of mind when you know that if your platform is bad at managing their money that they could be risking your investment too to the whims of bankruptcy court. The reason why this is an issue is because legally, you don't have a contract with the underlying investors, you have a contract with your platform. Every one of the platforms I recommend to you have this structure in place, except for lending club, which doesn't have one because it made it harder for them to get approved in all 50 states. However, lending club is the biggest player in the industry and has over a billion dollars in assets, as well as a backup-servicing plan, so I view it as a nonissue. It is something to consider nonetheless.

- Track record. Each one of these platforms has at least a couple years you can base data off of, which is important in this business. For example, banks require you to have a year or two of income you can prove so they see you can pay your mortgage. We should do the same with our investments.

You can also use peer to peer lending to invest in consumer loans through **Lending Club** and **Prosper**. Consumers refinance their credit card loans and auto loans, among other loans, through lending club, which allows people like you and I to fund the loans, with a minimum investment of 25 dollars. The returns tend to be in the 8-12 percent range if you do it right. The borrowers tend to be affluent, tech savvy, and carry a decent amount of consumer debt. In the Millionaire Trader series, there is a big section on lending club in *High Finance* by my colleague Logan C. Kane where he breaks down how robo advisors can improve returns in P2P lending. Lending Club is the biggest player in P2P, and they originate billions of dollars in loans, which they sell partially to Wall Street banks but also to ordinary investors through crowd funding. Prosper is like Lending Club's little brother, and they deal with a lot of borrowers who Lending Club might not approve, but are still considered to have good credit. Prosper has a bankruptcy remote structure, which is a big plus for peace of mind, whereas Lending Club does not. The main advantage of using LC over Prosper is that there is a secondary market for loans on LC, which gives you the means to sell most of your loans within a few weeks or so. If I only picked one between the two I would probably choose Prosper due to the greater peace of mind of the bankruptcy remote structure.

Lending Club and Prosper loans are for 3 or 5 year terms, and the borrowers pay monthly, paying you interest and principal every month that you can reinvest. You can invest in A+ credit borrowers all the way down to people at the edge of prime credit (640 FICO), some of them paying over 30 percent interest. Some will default, but if you diversify you should turn a really nice profit. It is really easy to diversify since the minimum investment is 25 dollars. If you invest in either LC or Prosper you should try to invest in at least 200 loans. This is a minimum investment of roughly 5,000 dollars either way. This makes it worthwhile to invest, and gives you a big enough sample size to see how you are doing.

P2P lending is a hot new trend that can deliver big returns to savvy investors, and I recommend playing it through Realty Shares, Peer Street, and Prosper. Lending Club is too big to ignore, and I encourage you to look at them too, even though I don't wholeheartedly recommend them. P2P lending can help you get some strong passive income, which you can use to take your financial life to the next level.

Semi-Absentee Businesses

I don't know about you, but I like the idea of being on vacation, drinking Coronas on the beach while I have a business open somewhere making me money to pay for my vacation. The right kind of business, run the right way, can provide a great potential for passive income and a high return. However, most business owners fail miserably at this task, because they choose the wrong kind of business. You can make a killing opening up a nice Italian restaurant with legitimately good food and a killer wine list, but when you own that kind of business, the business owns you. Now, you could have an awesome manager who takes care of things while you are away, but you need to have a profitable business to be able to pay the awesome manager the money he wants. If you don't have that, you are trapped. Also, many businesses are absolute minefields, with traps waiting for you in cash flow, inventory, receivables, and employee theft. What you need if you want passive income is the kind of business that is simple and easy to run, so you don't have to pay anyone else to do it. **This is called a semi-absentee business.** It is a fact that semi-absentee businesses fail at a much higher rate than manager owned businesses, but that is almost always because the business is too tricky for the management to handle, and the business has the wrong model for the owner and manager.

Characteristics of good semi-absentee businesses:

- Not a lot of inventory. Inventory is money, except you can't spend it, and until it moves, you don't' have money. If you own a restaurant, your inventory literally spoils if it isn't used. Not good. If you own a car dealership, you have millions of dollars of cars on the lot, and if you overpay for them, can't sell them, or have issues with your financier, you are out of business. Not good. Inventory makes it easy to screw up. On the other hand, if you own a business like a car wash, you don't have any inventory, unless you want to count soap. Other good businesses that can be run this way are auto repair places and laundromats. The common theme here is businesses that require equipment rather than inventory. This makes it much easier for you to be semi-passive.

- Not a lot of receivables. This applies especially to service businesses that tend to invoice on a 30-60 day schedule. If you own a business like this, you will spend a significant amount of time chasing down money from various people. This really kills the passivity part.
- Not highly regulated. Highly regulated industries, such as finance and insurance tend to have a lot of correspondence that needs to be responded to on a timely basis. Businesses like these need a sharp person to quarterback the operation, deal with

regulators, red tape, employees, etc.

Regulation makes your life hard, the less of it you have to deal with, the better.

You want to be able to focus on the strategy of your business, not the day-to-day tactics. Your goals as a semi-passive business owner are marketing, driving traffic, managing expenses, and ensuring that the people you have working for you are intelligent and trustworthy people. You can make a ton of money with the right business, but beware of businesses that people say are turnkey. Also, think very carefully and do plenty of due diligence before entering into a business, because you can't always pivot away from a business quickly just because things aren't working the way you thought. That said, here's a list of good businesses you can run semi-absentee, giving you a solid passive income, plus a short explanation of each. They are listed from most passive to least passive.

Publishing/Creating Art- Passivity grade A+
Nothing is more passive than creating art once, which sells over and over again. Musicians, actors, artists, writers, at least those who are successful, work once and get paid 100 times. That is as good as it gets from a passive income standpoint. Your copyright is for life in the US, plus 70 years. I will get paid from this book for the rest of my life. I like that! Another plus is that the startup cost is very minimal, as in 3 figures max.

Internet- Passivity grade A. Affiliate marketing, blogging, and similar businesses can be a huge moneymaker if you have skills in that area. Same as publishing, creation of art, startup cost is very low. You can make a website for free and start driving traffic to it within minutes, which you can monetize with AdSense, Amazon Associates, et cetera. Once you get it going, traffic tends to keep flowing, as does your cash flow.

Lending Money- Passivity grade A. The stock and bond markets would also score a 9 on this, but P2P gives you more control over your investments, which actually increases your passive income potential. You can also find other sources of people who want to borrow money and lend to them.

Real Estate- Passivity grade A if you have no mortgage, B+ if you have a mortgage. Real estate is as passive as a physical business can be if you have a good property manager who deals with tenants, collects rent, etc. Paying a mortgage puts a little more pressure on you, but it's still a pretty passive investment.

Car Washes and Laundromats- Passivity grade B+. As long as you have a good location and 2-3 employees who show up to work when they say they are going to you have a very passive business that can make upwards of 30-40k a month in the right location.

Vending Machines- Passivity grade B. Refill vending machines, get cash, repeat. It works even better if you have enough of them that you can hire other people to stock them for you, if you could take advantage of scale, then I would give it a B+.

Auto repair- Passivity grade B-. I'm including this one because of the high profit potential and the chances of getting a good manager/mechanic who you could split profits with. Auto repair places are fairly capital intensive, but good businesses nonetheless.

Franchises- Passivity grade C+. Your mileage is going to vary on this but some franchises are very good investments.

This isn't an exhaustive list of businesses with passive income potential, but it is a fantastic start. You now have 3 great sources of passive income that don't involve the stock market and have high returns. Your sources of great investments are real estate, P2P investments, and semi-absentee businesses. You may not agree with everything I write, but hopefully I helped you think a little outside the box when it comes to your money. I hope you enjoyed reading this book as much as I enjoyed writing it.

To sum everything up, you learned:

- How you can get started in real estate, the world's first great creator of wealth.
- How peer-to-peer investment platforms change the investing game, giving you access to consumer loans, real estate partnerships, and hard money loans.
- How real estate can shelter your income from taxes.
- How to select businesses that you can buy and run semi-absentee, giving you round the clock income.

Until next time,

Cameron Lancaster

www.ingramcontent.com/pod-product-compliance
Lightning Source LLC
Chambersburg PA
CBHW020708180526
45163CB00008B/2990